8/20

# This Bible belongs to

_____

_____

_____

Date _____

## Presented by

_____

*"Take courage; I have overcome the world."*

*St. Joseph*

# CATHOLIC
# CHILDREN'S BIBLE

———◆———

By
Rev. Lawrence G. Lovasik, S.V.D.
*Divine Word Missionary*

———◆———

*Illustrated*

**CATHOLIC BOOK PUBLISHING CORP.**
**New Jersey**

NIHIL OBSTAT: Francis J. McAree, S.T.D.
   *Censor Librorum*

IMPRIMATUR: ✠ Patrick J. Sheridan, D.D
   *Vicar General, Archdiocese of New York*

(T-145)

Copyright © 2000 Catholic Book Publishing Corp., N.Y.
Printed in Hong Kong

# CONTENTS

## The Old Testament

# The New Testament

# THE OLD TESTAMENT

Out of love, God made heaven and earth and the whole universe. He made Adam and Eve and called them to a life of perfect happiness.

When they did something God told them not to do, sin and sadness were known on earth for the first time. But God had a plan to save everyone.

He chose Abraham to be the father of a holy people. God protected His people and they became a mighty nation.

God prepared them for the day when He would send His only Son, Jesus, into the world. This was His plan of salvation!

# 1. GOD MAKES THE WORLD

"In the beginning God made the heavens and the earth."

He formed the hills and mountains, the rivers and seas, the clouds and the sky. He made the sun to light the day and the moon and stars to shine at night. And He made all kinds of plants and trees that had tasty fruit.

God filled the seas with fish and whales and made the birds that fly in the sky. And He brought forth animals that live on the land—sheep and cows that graze on the plains and the wild beasts of the forest.

Then God made human beings and told them to rule over the earth.

*Genesis 1*

## 2. ADAM AND EVE

God placed our first parents, Adam and Eve, in the beautiful Garden of Eden. They were very happy for they were close to God and were to live forever.

God told them not to eat the fruit of the Tree of Knowledge of good and evil. But Adam and Eve were tricked by the devil who appeared as a serpent and they disobeyed God.

Now they were sad and had to leave their beautiful garden. They would have to work hard for their food and would some day die.

God loved Adam and Eve, for He loves all people, and He promised to send a Redeemer Who would crush the power of the devil.

*Genesis 2*

# 3. NOAH'S ARK

As the human race grew, many people became wicked and disobeyed God.

There was a good man named Noah who loved God. God told him that soon a great flood would cover the earth. Noah should build an ark—a very large boat—and put his family in it. He should also lead pairs of all kinds of animals into the ark. Noah did as God said.

Then heavy rains flooded all the land. Every living thing—birds, animals, and people—drowned.

At last the rains stopped. So Noah came out of the ark with his family and all the living creatures.

Noah thanked God for saving his family. This pleased God very much.

*Genesis 6*

# 4. PROMISE TO ABRAM

God chose Abram to be the father of a new people. God told Abram to leave his country and to travel to a distant land. The Lord promised, "I will make of you a great nation. In you all people will be blessed."

Abram did as God said and went to the land of Canaan—the Promised Land. There God changed his name to Abraham which means, "father of many peoples."

Even though Abraham and his wife Sarah were very old, God gave them a son, Isaac.

And indeed all people were blessed through Abraham. From his family, many years later, the Redeemer would be born.

*Genesis 12; 15; 21*

# 5. PROMISE RENEWED TO JACOB

Isaac married Rebekah and God gave them twin boys named Esau and Jacob. Esau was jealous of Jacob, so Rebekah sent Jacob to visit an uncle who lived far away.

One day on his journey, Jacob was tired and fell asleep. He had a dream of a long ladder that reached up to heaven. Angels were going up and down the ladder.

Then God spoke, "The land that you are lying on I shall give to you and your children. In your children all nations of the earth shall be blessed."

When Jacob awoke, he called that place Bethel, which means "the house of God."

*Genesis 25*

# 6. JOSEPH AND HIS BROTHERS

Jacob had twelve sons and his favorite was Joseph. Out of jealousy, his brothers sold Joseph to some traders who took him to Egypt.

But God protected Joseph. God gave him the power to explain dreams. When Joseph explained the meaning of King Pharaoh's dream, the king put him in charge of the whole land.

Joseph's brothers came to Egypt to buy grain. Joseph sold it to them, but they did not know who he was. When his brothers came again, Joseph said, "I am your brother." Then Joseph wept and forgave them.

Joseph sent for his father. So Jacob and his whole family came to Egypt.

*Genesis 37*

# 7. BABY MOSES

A new king ruled in Egypt. He feared the Israelites for now they were a great number of people. So he made them slaves and forced them to work hard.

Then he ordered that every new-born Israelite boy was to be thrown into the river.

At this time Moses was born. His mother hid him in a basket placed at the river's edge, for they were Israelites.

When the king's daughter came to bathe in the river, she saw the basket. Just then the baby cried and this touched her heart.

She took the baby as her own and Moses was raised in Pharaoh's house.

*Exodus 1*

# 8. THE BURNING BUSH

One day Moses saw a strange sight—a bush was on fire but was not burning up.

God spoke to Moses from the bush. He told him that He was sending him to free the Israelites from slavery in Egypt. God said, "Go to the King of Egypt and tell him to let the Israelites go."

At first the king said no. Then God punished the land of Egypt with much suffering. So the king said to Moses, "Take your flocks and your people and leave Egypt."

Soon Pharaoh changed his mind and followed the Israelites with his army. Moses and the people were trapped between Pharaoh's army and the sea.

*Exodus 3*

# 9. GOD FREES HIS PEOPLE

Moses led the Israelites toward the Red Sea. When they saw Pharaoh's army coming after them, they were afraid.

But Moses knew that God was with them. He prayed for help. God told Moses to stretch his staff over the sea. Right away a mighty wind blew and it lasted all night. In the morning the waters were parted and a dry path appeared. All of Israel crossed the sea on dry land!

Then the Egyptians went in after them—horsemen, chariots, and horses. Moses lifted up his staff again and the waters rushed back covering all of Pharaoh's army. Not one was left.

*Exodus 13*

# 10. GOD FEEDS HIS PEOPLE

The Israelites set out across the desert. When the food that they had brought from Egypt was almost gone, they complained to Moses.

God told Moses that He would rain down bread for them from heaven. The next morning little white flakes, like frost, covered the sand around the camp. They tasted like bread made with honey. The people called this food "manna."

And in the evening God sent many birds, which they caught and ate.

God fed His people with manna in the desert for forty years until they came to the Promised Land.

God feeds us with true Bread from heaven each time we receive Holy Communion.

*Exodus 16*

# 11. THE COMMANDMENTS

One day Moses led the people out of camp to the foot of a mountain. Suddenly the mountain shook and God began to speak.

God called Moses to the top of the mountain. There He gave Moses Commandments, or rules, that the people were to follow. They were written on tablets of stone.

The people were to love God and respect His name. They should honor their parents. And they must never lie or hurt anyone. There were also other rules.

God promised the nation of Israel that if they obeyed Him, they would be His special people and He would be close to them.

*Exodus 19*

# 12. THE CITY OF JERICHO

After Moses died, God called Joshua to lead the Israelites into Canaan—the Promised Land. God showed Joshua how to capture the city of Jericho.

The walls of that city were very high and strong. How could the men of Israel enter it?

Joshua led the priests and people around the city in silence for six days. They carried the Ark of the Covenant—a golden chest in which the tablets of the Ten Commandments were kept.

On the seventh day, the priests blew their horns and the people gave a mighty shout. The walls of Jericho fell with a booming crash! And the Israelites captured the city.

*Joshua 1*

# 13. THE PROMISED LAND

There were many other strong cities like Jericho. And many kings with powerful armies fought against the Israelites. But God helped Joshua to defeat them all.

Now God's people lived in the Promised Land. Joshua divided the land among the twelve tribes of Israel.

He warned the people not to worship the idols of the nations near them. They must worship the God of Abraham, Isaac, and Jacob Who had been faithful to His promises.

The people told Joshua they would serve the Lord. And they prospered and grew strong.

From the tribe of Judah the Redeemer would be born.

*Joshua 8*

# 14. SAMUEL LEADS THE PEOPLE

When Samuel was four years old his mother Hannah took him to the Lord's shrine. Hannah was happy that God blessed her with a son. So she left Samuel there to serve God all his life.

One night God spoke to Samuel. God said that because Eli the priest and his sons were wicked, they would no longer be leaders in Israel. Samuel would take their place.

When Samuel was a man he warned the people to stop worshiping idols. He led many of them back to God.

God loved Samuel. Whenever he prayed for Israel's armies, God granted them victory.

*1 Samuel 1*

# 15.  ISRAEL'S FIRST KING

When Samuel was very old, the people asked him to give them a king like other nations.

Samuel prayed to God to help him choose the right person. Soon he saw a tall young man coming to meet him. Samuel knew he would be a fitting king. The man's name was Saul.

Then Samuel poured sacred oil on Saul's head. Samuel said, "God has anointed you king of the Israelites. You shall rule over them and protect them from their enemies."

Saul led the armies of Israel. God granted them victory as long as Saul was faithful to Him.

*1 Samuel 8*

# 16. DAVID AND GOLIATH

Saul called the armies of Israel together for the Philistines were about to attack. The Philistines had in their army a giant named Goliath.

Goliath challenged any soldier of Israel to fight him man to man to see who would win the war. But no Israelite dared to fight him.

David was only sixteen years old. He told Saul, "I will fight this giant. God will help me."

When Goliath came forth to meet him, David shot a stone from his sling. It struck Goliath right in the middle of his forehead and he fell to the ground.

The Philistines were amazed and fled in terror. Once again God protected His people.

*1 Samuel 17*

# 17. DAVID BECOMES KING

When Saul died, David became king. He made Jerusalem his capital city.

David wanted to lead the people to worship God as they should. So he brought the Ark of the Covenant to Jerusalem. He built a beautiful Tabernacle, or tent, to house the Ark.

The Ark was a sign of God's presence among His people. As the Ark entered Jerusalem, David and the people danced and sang for joy!

David was a good king and Israel became a great nation. David was also a poet. Inspired by God he wrote beautiful poems known as the Psalms.

God loved David and promised that the Redeemer would be born of his family.                    *2 Samuel 1*

# 18. SOLOMON'S TEMPLE

David's son Solomon was very young when he became king. Early in his rule, Solomon began to build a Temple to the Lord in Jerusalem. It was like the Tabernacle built in the desert. But it was much larger and was made of stone and cedar instead of a tent.

In the center of the Temple was the Holy of Holies. This was where the Ark was placed.

It took seven years to build the Temple. Only the finest wood and the purest gold were used. It was the most beautiful building ever seen.

God was pleased with the Temple. He gave a sign of His presence when a cloud filled the place where the Ark was kept.

*1 Kings 5*

# 19. PROPHETS SPEAK FOR GOD

When the people no longer served the Lord, He sent holy men to lead them back to Him. These were the prophets—special friends of God.

One day the prophet Isaiah in a vision saw the Lord on His throne with Angels serving Him. Isaiah felt unworthy to serve God. Suddenly an Angel touched his lips with a burning coal. Now he could speak for God.

God's loyal friend Jeremiah told the people that since they turned away from God, they would be led away as slaves by their enemies. But God would make them a great nation once more. The Redeemer would be their king.

*Isaiah 6; Jeremiah 2*

# 20.  THE EXILE

Soon after Solomon died, the nation of Israel was divided. The kingdom of Israel was in the north; in the south was the kingdom of Judah.

The people in Israel were not faithful to God. So He allowed them to be conquered by their enemies. They were carried off as slaves to a distant land. But God sent His prophets to remind them of His love. They should always hope in Him.

In Judah also, the people did not serve God. Their enemies conquered Jerusalem and set fire to the Temple. The people had to leave their homes. They were slaves in a strange land. But God sent His prophets to help them find their way back to Him.

*1 Kings 17*

## 21.  RETURN TO JERUSALEM

The people were slaves in foreign lands for about seventy years. Then they returned to their own country.

Nehemiah was given permission to rebuild the City of Jerusalem. At first he built a wall around the city.

Then he began to rebuild the Temple on the same place where Solomon's Temple stood. And the people celebrated the opening of the Temple with great joy.

*Isaiah 40*

# THE NEW TESTAMENT

This part of the Bible is the story of Jesus, the Son of God. We read how Jesus spent His whole life doing good. He healed sick people, made blind people see, and raised to life those who had died.

He did these things because He loves us. These wonderful deeds also show that He has power over sin and death because He was sent by the Father.

By His life, death, and rising, Jesus helps us to be His brothers and sisters—true children of God.

He trusted this message to His Apostles and to the Church they founded.

God sent the Holy Spirit to guard and guide His people until Jesus comes again.

# 1. THE ANGEL SPEAKS TO MARY

Now the time had come—the Redeemer would soon be here.

Gabriel, one of God's chief Angels, was sent to speak to a young girl named Mary. She lived in Nazareth and was soon to be married to Joseph.

The Angel said, "God has chosen you to be the mother of a Son. You shall call Him Jesus. He will rule the people forever."

Mary was not sure how this would come about. But she loved God very much and always placed her trust in Him.

So Mary said, "Let it be done to me as you say." And she became mother of the Redeemer.

*Luke 1*

# 2. MARY VISITS ELIZABETH

Mary had a cousin, Elizabeth. She and her husband Zechariah always wanted a child. Now they were old and would be alone.

But God heard their prayers and they would soon have a son named John. Mary learned of this from the Angel Gabriel, so she went to help her cousin.

When Elizabeth saw Mary, she was filled with joy and cried out, "Blest are you among women."

Mary cleaned, cooked, and cared for Elizabeth until her child was born. For Mary always thought of others.

When John grew up, he pointed out the Redeemer to the people.

*Luke 1*

# 3. JESUS IS BORN

Mary and Joseph were tired after the long journey from Nazareth to Bethlehem. It was hard to find a place to rest. But Joseph found a stable where they would be sheltered from the cold.

That very night Mary's Child was born. He was so beautiful! Soon He was asleep in Mary's arms. Mary and Joseph were filled with joy as they beheld Him.

The Angels in heaven were watching. And an Angel appeared to shepherds in the fields. The Angel said, "I bring you good news of great joy. This night in the City of David a Savior has been born."

Suddenly the sky was filled with Angels who were praising and thanking God.

# 4. THREE WISE MEN

Shortly after Jesus was born, three Wise Men came to Jerusalem. In the East where they lived, a bright star appeared in the sky. It was a sign that a new king had been born in Judea and they wanted to honor him.

Herod was ruler in Judea and he feared any new king. So he told the Wise Men to find the Child and report to him.

The Wise Men once again followed the star. It led them to the Child and His mother Mary. Then they worshiped Him and gave Him precious gifts.

In a dream God warned them not to go back to Herod. So they returned to their country by another way.

*Matthew 2*

# 5. THE BOY JESUS

Mothers always worry. One time Mary worried. Here is what happened.

When Jesus was twelve years old, He went to Jerusalem with Mary and Joseph. When the holiday was over, His parents started home and found out that Jesus was not with them.

For three days they searched for Him. At last they found Jesus in the Temple. He was listening to the Teachers and asking questions. Everyone was surprised at His learning.

When Mary told Him how worried they were, Jesus said, "Did you not know I must be in My Father's house?"

They returned together to Nazareth, and Mary was happy again.

*Luke 2*

# 6. JESUS IS BAPTIZED

The time finally came when Jesus was about thirty years old to leave His home in Nazareth and begin His Father's work.

He went to the region near the Jordan river. His cousin John was preaching there, calling the people back to God. John also baptized them.

When Jesus asked John to baptize Him, John said, "It is I who should be baptized by You." But Jesus told him to go ahead.

As Jesus came out of the water, John saw the Holy Spirit come down upon Him in the form of a dove.

Then a voice from heaven said, "This is My beloved Son." Now John knew, and he told the people that Jesus was the Son of God!

*Matthew 3*

# 7. JESUS CHANGES WATER INTO WINE

One day Mary was invited to a wedding feast. Jesus and His special friends went with her.

There was plenty of food to eat and wine to drink. Everyone was happy.

But later Mary noticed that the wine ran out and she told Jesus. Jesus had the waiters fill six big jars with water. Then He said, "Now pour out what you need and take it to the head waiter to taste." Only then was it known that Jesus had turned the water into wine!

This was the first of His wonderful deeds called miracles. Jesus did them as signs of His power as Son of God.

*John 2*

# 8. JESUS CHOOSES THE APOSTLES

Jesus began to preach the Gospel—the good news of God's great love for us. Many people went to hear Him.

Some became His special friends and helpers. From these Jesus chose twelve men who would share His life in a special way. They were called Apostles.

Jesus sent them to the towns with power to cure sick people. They did other marvelous things in Jesus' name.

He made the Apostles the first priests of His Church. They received power to offer Mass, forgive sins, and teach in His name. They would take His place on earth and pass on their special gifts to other priests.

*Matthew 10*

# 9. JESUS TEACHES THE PEOPLE

More and more people wanted to hear Jesus preach. The crowds grew so large that one day He climbed up on a hill so all could see and hear Him.

He told them that they would be blest if they were poor in spirit; they were humble; they were sorry for sins; they were pure; they were peacemakers; they were willing to suffer for God.

Jesus also taught them to trust in God when they prayed, to forgive their enemies, and to try to be holy. Then they would truly be children of God.

*Matthew 5*

# 10. JESUS HEALS

In the Bible there are many stories about Jesus healing the sick. He did this to take away their pain and help them be happy. These acts also showed His power as Son of God.

One story tells about a man who could not move. His friends brought him to the house where Jesus was teaching. So many people wanted to hear Jesus that no one could get in the door.

But his friends had a great idea. They opened a hole in the roof and lowered him down near Jesus.

Jesus told the man that his sins were forgiven. Then He said, "Get up, pick up your mat and walk." He was cured at once, picked up his mat, and walked away!

*Mark 2*

# 11. JESUS RESTORES LIFE

Soon afterward Jesus and His followers went to the town of Naim. There they met a funeral procession. The only son of a widow was to be buried.

Jesus was moved with pity as He saw the mother's sorrow. He said to her, "Don't cry."

Then He touched the coffin and said, "Young man, I tell you, arise." The young man sat up and began to speak. And Jesus gave him to his mother.

The people watching were filled with fear. They knew that only God, the Giver of life, could raise a dead person back to life.

In this way once again, Jesus showed that He was the Son of God.

*Luke 7*

# 12. JESUS FEEDS THE PEOPLE

It was a long day. The large crowd listened to Jesus for many hours. Now they were hungry.

When the Apostles asked Jesus to send the people home, He said, "You can give them food to eat." For Jesus knew what He was going to do.

They had five loaves of bread and two dried fish. Jesus took the loaves and fish into His hands. He blessed them and told the Apostles to give them to the people—there were over five thousand! And they all ate as much as they wanted.

When the people saw how Jesus had fed them with so little food, they wanted to make him king. But Jesus hid from them.

*John 6*

# 13. JESUS SHOWS HIS GLORY

Jesus is really God and really Man. When He lived on earth, He looked like other men. For His Man-ness was clearly seen but His God-ness was hidden. But one special day He showed His glory.

That day Jesus went up a high mountain with Peter, James, and John. Suddenly His face became as bright as the sun and His clothes were whiter than snow. Moses and Elijah appeared and spoke with Him.

Then a voice from heaven said, "This is My beloved Son; listen to Him."

Jesus let the three Apostles see His heavenly glory so they would remember that He is God even though He would soon suffer on the Cross.

*Matthew 17*

# 14. JESUS BLESSES THE CHILDREN

Jesus loved little children. One day some mothers brought their children to Him to be blessed.

The Apostles, knowing that Jesus was tired, tried to keep the children away.

But Jesus told them, "Let the children come to Me. Do not stop them." Children were not a bother to Him. They were His special joy.

Then Jesus said to the grown-ups, "Unless you change and become like little children, you will never enter the Kingdom of Heaven."

Jesus wants us to imitate little children in the way they are so trustful, have hearts full of hope, and are always ready to share their love.

*Mark 9*

# 15. JESUS SHOWS US HOW TO LOVE

One day Jesus told a story. Robbers sprang out of the bushes and grabbed a man. Then they beat him, stole everything he had, and left him lying on the road.

Soon a priest came near. He saw the man but did not stop. A Levite on the road also hurried by.

But a Samaritan saw him and, moved with pity, stopped to wash his wounds. Then he took the man to an inn and cared for him.

Of the three, only the Samaritan treated the man as a neighbor and helped him in his need.

Jesus told this story to teach us how to love. When we help our brothers and sisters who are in need, we are like the Good Samaritan.

*Luke 10*

# 16. THE PEOPLE WELCOME JESUS

Great crowds followed Jesus wherever He went. They had been told about His wonderful works and wanted to hear Him speak.

His enemies feared that all the people would believe in Him. Then they would lose their power. Soon His enemies would have their day, but this day was a triumph for Jesus.

Jesus was going to Jerusalem once more. As He rode into the city on a donkey, the people cut down branches from the trees and spread them in His path. Others waved palms.

And they shouted greetings, "Hosanna to the Son of David. Blessed is He Who comes in the name of the Lord."

*Matthew 21*

# 17. A SPECIAL MEAL

For a long time Jesus had planned this special meal. He would soon be put to death. This would be His Last Supper with the Apostles.

While they were eating, Jesus took bread, blessed it, and broke it, and said, "Take and eat, this is My Body."

Then He took a cup of wine, gave thanks, and gave it to them, saying, "Drink from it, all of you, for this is My Blood. Do this in memory of Me."

Thus Jesus gave His Apostles His Body and Blood in Communion. And He gave them the power to give Communion to others by making them His first priests. These special friends would take His place on earth and be "other Christs" until He comes again.

*Mark 14*

# 18. JESUS DIES ON THE CROSS

The enemies of Jesus were afraid that the whole nation would believe in Him. So they had Him condemned to die on a cross.

When He was nailed to the Cross, Jesus prayed, "Father forgive them; they do not know what they are doing." And as His last gift, He gave us all His own dear mother Mary to be our mother.

And it seemed as if even nature wept. The sun became dark and the earth shook with rumbling thunder.

Then in a loud voice, Jesus cried, "Father into Your hands I commend My spirit." And He died.

The sinless One died so that sinners might live.

*Luke 23*

# 19. HE IS RISEN!

All was quiet, silent, hushed. The soldiers guarding Jesus' tomb were glad the night was over. It was Sunday morning.

Mary Magdalene and her friends were going to the tomb to anoint the Body.

All at once the earth trembled. An Angel came down from heaven and rolled back the stone in front of the tomb. The guards, shaken with fear, fell to the ground.

Then the Angel said to the women, "I know you are seeking Jesus the crucified. He is not here, for He has been raised."

The women were filled with joy. And they ran to tell the Apostles the wonderful news—He is risen!

*Matthew 28*

## 20. JESUS APPEARS TO THE APOSTLES

Now it was evening of the day Jesus rose from the dead. The Apostles were together in the upper room.

Suddenly Jesus stood among them. "Peace be with you," He said.

Some thought He was a ghost; so He let them feel Him. And He showed them the wounds in His hands and feet.

Then He breathed on them and said, "Receive the Holy Spirit. If you forgive people's sins, they are forgiven." Thus Jesus gave them and their successors the power to forgive sins in the Sacrament of Penance.

The Apostles were filled with joy. All their sadness was gone. Hope came back into their hearts. *John 20*

# 21. JESUS ASCENDS TO HEAVEN

Finally the day came when Jesus would return to the Father. Forty days had passed since He rose from the dead. Now He led the Apostles to a mountain in Galilee.

Then He told them, "Go and make believers of all nations, baptizing them in the name of the Father, and of the Son, and of the Holy Spirit. Teach them to observe all that I have told you."

As Jesus lifted His hands to bless them, He began to rise higher and higher in the sky until they could see Him no more.

The Apostles rejoiced and returned to Jerusalem to await the coming of the Holy Spirit.

*Matthew 28*

# 22. THE HOLY SPIRIT COMES

When the Apostles returned to Jerusalem, they spent much time in prayer. They gathered together in the upper room with Mary the mother of Jesus.

It was now ten days since Jesus ascended to heaven. Suddenly a loud sound like a mighty wind filled the whole house. And tongues of fire came down upon each one. They were filled with the Holy Spirit.

Peter went out and preached to a vast crowd. He spoke so lovingly about Jesus that many people were deeply moved and were baptized.

Now the Apostles, strengthened by the Holy Spirit, went forth and joyously proclaimed the Good News.

*Acts 2*

# 23. JESUS LEAVES US THE CHURCH

Shortly after Jesus had chosen His Apostles, He had said that Peter would be the rock upon whom He would build His Church.

After they received the Holy Spirit, the Apostles went out into the world telling the people about Jesus. And the number of believers grew day by day. Before long the Gospel was proclaimed to all the world.

Today the pope, who is the successor to Peter, shepherds the Church from the Vatican in Rome.

Jesus will be with His Church until the end of time. And He constantly intercedes for us in heaven.

And Jesus sent the Holy Spirit to guard and guide His Church until He comes again. *Matthew 16*

## PRAYER OF THANKS FOR
## THE BIBLE

Heavenly Lord,
thank You for giving us the
Bible,
which is Your Word to us.

It is the written story
of Your actions in the world;
let me read my Bible stories often.

Help me to know You better,
love You more,
and get closer to You.

96

# Other Great Books for Children

**OUR HEAVENLY MOTHER**—New beautiful large-size book of the three greatest appearances of Our Lady on earth—at Guadalupe, Lourdes, and Fatima. **Ask for No. 272**

The **STORY OF JESUS**—By Father Lovasik, S.V.D. A large-format book with magnificent full color pictures for young readers to enjoy and learn about the life of Jesus. Each story is told in simple and direct words. **Ask for No. 535**

**FIRST BOOK OF SAINTS**—By Father Lovasik, S.V.D. A magnificent full-color book about the Saints, featuring a full-page illustration of each Saint. **Ask for No. 133**

**LIVES OF THE SAINTS**—New Revised Edition. Short life of a Saint and prayer for every day of the year. Over 50 illustrations. Ideal for daily meditation and private study. **Ask for No. 870**

**PICTURE BOOK OF SAINTS**—By Rev. L. Lovasik, S.V.D. Illustrated Lives of the Saints in full color for Young and Old. It clearly depicts the lives of over 100 popular Saints in word and picture. **Ask for No. 235**

**PICTURE BOOK OF PRAYERS**—New beautiful book of prayers for children featuring prayers for the day, major feasts, various occasions, and special days: First Communion, Confirmation, Name Day, and Birthday. **Ask for No. 265**

**MY FRIENDS THE SAINTS**—By Father Lovasik, S.V.D. New beautiful large-size book of the most popular Saints that children will love to read. It contains short biographical details as well as inspiring prayers. **Ask for No. 270**

*WHEREVER CATHOLIC BOOKS ARE SOLD*